Seasons

First published 2020 by The Hedgehog Poetry Press

Published in the UK by
The Hedgehog Poetry Press
5, Coppack House
Churchill Avenue
Clevedon
BS21 6QW

www.hedgehogpress.co.uk

ISBN: 978-1-913499-40-2
Copyright © Katie Proctor 2020

The right of Katie Proctor to be identified as the author of this work has been asserted in accordance with the Copyright, Designs and Patents Act 1988.

All rights reserved. No part of this publication may be reproduced, stored in or introduced into a retrieval system, or transmitted in any form, or by any means (electronic, mechanical, photocopying, recording or otherwise) without prior written permissions of the publisher. Any person who does any unauthorised act in relation to this publication may be liable for criminal prosecution and civil claims for damages.

9 8 7 6 5 4 3 2 1

A CIP Catalogue record for this book is available from the British Library.

Seasons

by

Katie Proctor

Contents

twin flame / twin fish 7

Firsts 8

Distant 9

Lucid 10

Lemon and Ginger Tears 11

Can You Find These? 12

Better Tuesdays 13

an empty infinity 14

The thing about destiny 15

Victims 16

What she called love 17

spring-time / summer-time 18

Seasons 19

Acknowledgements 22

twin flame / twin fish

you said we were written in outer space.
i always wondered if it was ever that simple –
if there was really something that existed
long before all of us. tracing the milky way, planning us out.
putting the stars in their places, filling gaps
in the jigsaws of our bodies we pretend to understand.
purpose-built ignition, a maze of brainwaves.
someone who knew us before we knew ourselves.
knowing that i was meant to be an astrological explosion,
an asteroid set to cause a scene. predestined to fill
the empty space with life.
and now i wonder why we ever believed that
we were twin flames in my world of water.
why i ever told myself i could settle for anything less
than a soulmate. why i ever thought i could be pushed into
equilibrium when i was born to be off-kilter,
tipped out of control by a whisper. a kaleidoscope
of emotions made only for me, when planets aligned
in some sort of miracle. a mystery. a constellation of eclecticism.

Firsts

You were salt and vinegar fingers. Feather light touches, a trail of heat, searing heat, enflaming. Bleeding red lips. Eyes sewn shut. Choking down a sound that rises from somewhere you weren't sure existed. Learning contours like an equation. Sneaking touches in the car on the way home. Hands dancing around each other. A game, a game of pretend. Pretending like we have no idea what we're doing. Pretending like we don't risk everything for five minutes alone together. Me sitting on the sinks, you on the windowsill. Launching into a conversation we've picked apart at the seams, rehearsed until it fell apart. Not even knowing we liked it. The flushed cheeks, the shaking hands, the game of pretend. Not even knowing why we're tangled up in each other's honesty. Why one of us is locking the door, the other closing the blinds. Why we force ourselves closer, spurred on by some kind of desperation. Using the wrong words on purpose, falling into a well-practiced faux pas, making conversation without meaning so we get seconds more. Taking what we can get. Not thinking. Just touching. Making our numbered days feel like they'll last forever until finally we run out. Tracing the same circles. Kissing the same lips. Wondering if this is really what I was waiting for. Knowing nothing will ever be quite like this again.

Distant

In my dreams I am sitting by my window
as it rains outside, and
you are here beside me.
You, with your hair all around you
on the sheets, covered in the stars
and moonlight. You are laughing.
I wonder distantly what it would take
to feel your skin pressed to mine -
perhaps a fee paid in train tickets
and Polaroid photos, a notebook
with flowers from your hometown
pressed between the pages.
I think about what it would be like
to be immortalised with you
in words forever. A haiku
made from paintbrushes, and
the scent of the meadow where we
are sitting from sunrise to sunset.
when I wake I am sitting by my window
as it rains outside, and
you are here beside me.
You, with your letters stamped and
waiting for me, covered in the stars
and moonlight. I hope you are laughing too.

Lucid

I stay awake dreaming. Lucid. Shades of red, pink, kissing in alleyways. Fingers brushing as we talk, laughing, glances a little too long to be labelled friendly. I spent hours weaving my fears around yours until they melt away. Pauses in the cold like the films when the rain starts falling, running down the cobbled streets. Not caring when the damp starts soaking through my tights. Standing. Our eyes inches apart. Neither of us knowing what to say or do. Giggling. Lips meeting clumsily. Dynamite behind a door. And everything just shatters. And there's nothing inside me that says no. And we stand there, feeling, maybe loving. Wondering. Letting butterflies escape from our mouths. And it's funny. I never thought no strings attached really existed until I met you. But I swear I wouldn't even care if you just kissed me and said that was all you wanted. If you let me feel those electrics, see those city lights in the colour I've been missing for so long. I think I've found the right person. And I'm meant to feel like I'm flying. She's meant to open me up because she wants to pick apart my insecurities. She's meant to look at me like the world ends tomorrow. Our fingers are meant to be tangled, and we're not meant to pull away. It's meant to feel like the rest of the universe is on fire, and we're at the centre of it all. She is a galaxy, light years away from me. Yet I stay awake, my fantasies exploding in the sky. My tears lighting up my skin. Phosphorescence on a rainy day. The moon pulls me in and out. I still cry her name.

Lemon and Ginger Tears

You are a web of contradictions,
connected by broken promises
and songs you let kill you
in the back seat of your car.
Chaos coated in concealer,
a shell of glitter glue
and silver sparkle.
You sleep in sarcasm
till it haunts you, drinking in
pretence hoping desperately
he'll see through the mask you
replace with careful hands every
single morning.
When it's midnight, and you dream
of your teeth falling out
one by one,
against the sound of rain hitting the
window, and you wish he was there
to put them back where they came from.
You drown yourself in midweek
drinking, lemon and ginger tears among
silenced screams in the upstairs bathroom.
And your eyes cry cranberry
but someone else wants
to take you home – do you want
to keep them waiting?

Can You Find These?

I stopped going to counselling
because I couldn't answer this question.
If I could find them, I wouldn't be here.
Sitting in the same red chair,
looking at the same books
on the same shelf.
Dodging your eyes and filling
the silence with something new
because I couldn't bear to be asked
to look inside myself again.
Because I've done far too much searching
and found far too few answers.
I can't find them.
Maybe they were never inside me
or maybe he took them away when
I learnt how to be scared of a thing that should have been safe.
When I forgot what safety meant,
and when minutes turned into hours,
into days of being paralysed
by everything he was and
everything I wanted him to be.
Can you find these?
If I could, I would have stopped coming.
But I can't, and I stopped coming anyway.

Better Tuesdays

My bed is cold with the memory of the night before
You slipped from my grasp
still hot
on my skin
and I am emptily alone in the
dark dreaming better Tuesdays
Your name falls from my lips
honey-soaked / caramel-coated
a sunrise prayer of slenderness
I will pick flowers in a
champagne flute
Lay the glass at your feet
and mountains will move
with the weight of my heart
Yet still you are otherworldly
Bleeding in the palest blue
your breath comes in stains
Alternate lovers
dreaming better Tuesdays

an empty infinity

Do you remember when
we didn't know our days were numbered?
The sun was out and we danced
like it was forever.
Goodbyes didn't stretch out like
ever-collapsing dreams, perpetual,
unrelenting.
Before's temporaries became today's
permanents and we burned,
kindred spirits, soulmates.
And everything we ever believed in
seemed to come alight and dance
among the trees, my heart and yours;
intertwined, incandescent.
Yet the world has paused its spin
and its axis has rusted, and
we are frozen, nothing but
a microscope slide
in this melted endlessness, an
empty infinity.

The thing about destiny

I broke you like a habit / like the truths that leaked / from the corner of my wavering lips / and dripped into your hands / stinking of vulnerability / meant nothing more than a mistake / because I didn't know what else to do
I think we were waiting / for something to fill the empty space / for our memories to split / and bleed across the ocean / because we needed something that would make it all better again / and what better than the feeling / of when you put your trust / in something that would talk back / and the world didn't end / but instead you were dynamite / head to toe / and suddenly something made sense
What else would fix things / what better to make love feel alive again / than that moment when you swore / you would never be the same again / and for once you believed it was possible / to twist your faith around mine / stand back and watch it go off in the sky / a pyrotechnical promise to everyone / waiting to feel the same way
Would you have listened if I said / that maybe there's nothing out there / carving our names into the sky / making the angels believe we were star-crossed
Would you have listened if I told you / I never believed we were meant to be

Victims

You made me shatter / and I was in pieces / mirror shards / your protestations staring / back at you from the floor / where you couldn't help but throw me / like I was nothing / but a plaything to twist / into a victim
So sometimes I take myself back / and pretend like I'm who I was / before I opened my arms to you / but the truth is I'll never have the / bright eyes you pierced between your fingernails / without care / because you said they were so pretty
But explosions don't come without aftermath / and the proof will always be where / you left it / because you have never been more wrong / than when you thought you would escape / in your nonchalance
I like to think / I know your guilt
I know the darkest parts of you / and I know my memory still lives / somewhere you don't want to address / so you'll act like it's fine / that I disappeared because you / couldn't stop blaming me
You will cover your wounds / with plasters too small / and you will tell yourself / you were right all along
Pretence does not prove anything / and that is a promise because / I am not a saint / and I have screwed things up too / but I have changed and I / would let myself collapse / before papering over the cracks / with lies that will only fracture
Let me tell you / you will not stay sane / as long as you cannot grow
I do not search for a sorry / and I do not plead for you / on your knees / but I ask you / learn / do not look to be a hero / before you have been a victim / to your own mistakes

What she called love

It was strange that I thought
she had given me the world.
Said she had opened my eyes
to what was truly inside me,
the abyss that nobody but her
could stand to see,
but she peeled open
full of grins and eager eyes,
ripped apart the finest parts of me
and convinced me I was
selfish under the sunshine shell.
Funny how she laughed
like it was a miracle that
suddenly I hated myself.
She lifted each limb by a thread,
pushed my body every which way
until I was exactly what she wanted,
and I learnt to believe
that love was just one person
who wanted something from another
and would do whatever they could
to get it.
But when I walked away
she spilled out of my skin.
The sea rose around me,
the butterflies flocked to the sunshine shell.
And suddenly
I knew where the darkness had come from all along.

spring-time / summer-time

Do you remember when I thought
love only existed in the pages
of my textbook, and your
biro scribbles? And nothing would
ever match up to you and
all my dreams in technicolour.
When a word from you sent me
spiralling, some kind of ecstasy
and some kind of terror, lethal,
straight to the heart. You were
my shot at the night,
my one last chance that was never
really the end,
until it was. Did you see it, do you
see it now? I've outgrown you
after all this time. A seed
in the spring-time, planted by another's
hands in your shape. But blooming
without you forever, solitary
in the summer-time.

Seasons

The worst people for you
are the ones who look so captivating

You will always
fall this hard

do not seek to change it

Pick their words out from the
fabric of your being
with those tender fingers
They are not weaved into your skin

Close your mind to those
who tell you they will remain
it will happen if you let it

Nobody ever tells you
that a person like that cannot stay
sewn into a person like you

Do not try to mix black with white
you will only find grey

It is not yours to question
whether you were enough
you were so much
they took parts of you
from your grasp

Stop believing they had the right
what they took
they stole

they searched the depths of you
the places you hide till sunset
with probing hands that do not wait
to hear a confirmation

Their untruths might have left
a heart so empty you fear
it will never love again

but when the spring comes again
you will heal
and you will bloom

and it will be brighter
than they ever were

Acknowledgements

Thank you to all the writers who have inspired me – there are too many to name. I feel so incredibly grateful to be around so many talented people who constantly encourage me to be the best poet and person I can be.

Thank you to my family and my friends for their endless support of my work. I will always consider myself to be the luckiest person alive whilst I have you in my life.

Thank you to everyone reading this. I hope it resonates, and thank you for making it this far. I appreciate you.

Seasons was originally published by HEALer Magazine and rose quartz magazine in 2019.

Firsts was originally published by rose quartz magazine in 2019.

Victims was originally published by Clitbait in 2019.

www.ingramcontent.com/pod-product-compliance
Lightning Source LLC
Chambersburg PA
CBHW021455080526
44588CB00009B/866